M-A-C-N-O-L-I-A

ALSO BY A. VAN JORDAN

Rise

M-A-C-N-O-L-I-A

POEMS

A. Van Jordan

W. W. NORTON & COMPANY

New York London

For information about permission to reproduce selections from this book, write to
Permissions, W. W. Norton & Company, Inc., 500 Fifth Avenue, New York, NY 10110

Manufacturing by Courier Westford
Book design by JAM Design
Production manager: Anna Oler

Library of Congress Cataloging-in-Publication Data
Jordan, A. Van
M-A-C-N-O-L-I-A / A. Van Jordan.— 1st ed.
p. cm.
ISBN 0-393-05907-3 (hardcover)
1. African American teenage girls—Poetry. 2. Spelling bees—Poetry. I. Title: MacNolia.
II. Title.
PS3610.O654M33 2004
811'.6—dc22

2004002567

ISBN 0-393-32764-7 pbk.

W. W. Norton & Company, Inc., 500 Fifth Avenue, New York, N.Y. 10110
www.wwnorton.com

W. W. Norton & Company Ltd., Castle House, 75/76 Wells Street, London W1T 3QT

3 4 5 6 7 8 9 0

for Miles Kenneth Slack,

so you'll be ready

Contents

M-A-C-N-O-L-I-A

"MacNolia Cox Montiere, of 189 W. North St., died
September 12 at St. Thomas Hospital. Born in Kenmore,
she had been a lifetime resident of Akron. She was a member
of Livingstone Baptist Church. She won the *Beacon Journal*
Akron Spelling Bee in 1936. She is survived by husband,
John. . . ."

Obituary, Akron *Beacon Journal*
September 14, 1976

John Montiere

"Mercy, Mercy, Mercy"

September 12, 1976

INTERIOR—NIGHT—Panning shot of MACNOLIA's
bedroom on her deathbed.

The melody seeps through her room
Like a bad man's walk, something sexy
In one step, something sinister
In the other. The bed's bones creak as

Death slips under the sheets. Nightstands
At either side of her headboard hold
Her combs, while the sun cries mercy
At 7:00 p.m. She looks up scared

From her book's curled, yellow pages
As the room fills with staccato breaths
From Adderley's reed. My eyes melt
Under my tongue's flame as I stand

At the door of her room. She sees
Me now and looks out again. Her lips
Curl like dry, burning leaves into
A smile and her fingers trace half notes

In the air. Am I water drawn
For your bath? Am I the needle's cry
Across the album's grooves? Am I
This song's moan over your moist body?

INTERIOR—DAY—Flashback to JOHN's father. Soft shot.

In September, like this September,
Long ago, my sand-skinned father,
The steel worker, turned up my collar
On my one white shirt and twirled his

Hands into a silk, brown Windsor knot.
A figure rising, or coming
Home, at sunup and passing me, his
Punch to the shoulder I held all

Day, his open hand on my mother's
Face I held all night . . . I am my
Young eyes blazing scenes in the dark, his
Son sorting the language of his

Touch, which taught me of the twin angels,
Joy and pain, asleep in a man's
Palms, always awakened by those whom
He owes so much. Don't ask where I

Learned to soothe a dying woman's last
Days with these hands, ask why I am
Afraid, even now, to let her fly.

after Philip Levine

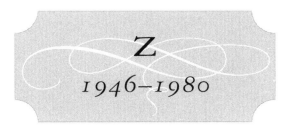

Z

1946–1980

"That's all he really wanted out of life, was love . . . how he
lost it. You see, he just didn't have any to give."

Jedediah Leland to Charles Foster Kane
Citizen Kane

"My guitar is mine, and I can play it how I want."

Conchita Perez to Mathieu Faber
That Obscure Object of Desire

in · cho · ate (♥) *adj.* Only begun or entered upon; incipient. As when ribbons of light peer through *inchoate* air, before the thought of loss or love come into focus, as when the first glance of a stranger brushes over you, and, for that breath of time, you wonder if time has double-crossed you; you wonder if this could be the start of a new ending, or if this look—this probe up your spine, this eye on your leg, neck, lips, hair—could come from a ghost of someone—someone, mind you, who you thought you deserved; someone, mind you, who taught you how not to love— whose hand opens like your mouth once did while saying, with innocence, *Yes,* over and over again.

John Montiere *answer to question one*

I taught Mac [sic] how to drink and she was no longer as I remembered her to be: she was no longer quiet and steady and quick-to-answer. She was no longer not ready to surrender; she had surrendered. She had only crumbs of her past: she worked hard, but she hated work; she knew all the answers on game shows, but she would never compete; she had a shy smile, but she laughed like a man. Her eyes no longer looked like the dark wells I would fall into when we first met; her eyes were bottomless pits filled with sadness, dark holes I feared. I could no longer look at myself in those eyes.

If I would look into her eyes, it was as if fingers would strip off my clothes, and I would want to strip off my skin, but I'd fear it would not help my fear; it may only lead to my bones, without the distraction of my flesh to comfort me.

John

The Moment Before He Asks
MacNolia Out on a Date

Look at her.
I can tell she has never
Drunk from the same glass
Of a man whose palm played
On her bare thigh,
Stunning the skin
Till her bones danced
Beneath his fingers.

Just look at her.

When this girl—with eyes so brown
They undermine sunrises
Over this dirty city—tilts her head up
From her book
And peeks into my own
Black sockets, I wonder

Will she see the empty spaces
Left between us
By the words I strain
For to ask the simplest questions:
Have you ever felt a man beg with his eyes?
Baby, have you ever seen flames struggle through twilight?

Naw, I can look at her shoes,
Scuffs on her heels,
And know. I can
Look at any woman's walk,
How her arms swing;
Or, for that matter, the way
She holds her purse,
Like a sack of potatoes
Or a child's hand;
The way she sits,
Legs crossed at the ankles
Or thighs pried open,
And I can tell all I need to know.

Meeting John Montiere

Blue tie, blue suit, blue shoes, cuff links, cigar,
And a child's grin pokes through his face, forces
The despair lodged beneath his eyes to lift.
Everything is blue except his eyes and the sky:
Both strain under the weight of night,
While night strains under a bracelet of stars.
So much darkness, so much light—I can't tell
Which looks more in need, which I desire more:
His smile or the sunset. A stillness, then
He raises my head from my book; not with his
Hands, but his stare, which could twist steel,
Brings me to his face. I'm a firefly blooming in a jar.
    So many words hover around my head . . .
    It's hard to hear what he says for the words.

John

Rant

nicked skin, I spill blood
now to show the life in me.
dance, cry, glance, crawl, starve,
tongue, flesh, swarm, trap—girl, see: men
don't need no big words to beg.

from (⇨) *prep.* 1. Starting at (a particular place or time): As in, John was *from* Chicago, but he played guitar straight *from* the Delta; he wore a blue suit *from* Robert Hall's; his hair smelled like coconut; his breath, like mint and bourbon; his hands felt like they were *from* slave times when he touched me—hungry, stealthy, trembling. 2. Out of: He pulled a knot of bills *from* his pocket, paid the man and we went upstairs. 3. Not near to or in contact with: He smoked the weed, but, surprisingly, he kept it *from* me. He said it would make me too self-conscious, and he wanted those feelings as far away *from* us as possible; he said a good part of my beauty was that I wasn't conscious of my beauty. Isn't that funny? So we drank Bloody Mothers (Hennessey and tomato juice), which was hard to keep *from* him—he always did like to drink. 4. Out of the control or authority of: I was released *from* my mama's house, *from* dreams of hands holding me down, *from* the threat of hands not pulling me up, *from* the man that knew me, but of whom I did not know; released *from* the dimming of twilight, *from* the brightness of morning; *from* the love I thought had to look like love; *from* the love I thought had to taste like love, *from* the love I thought I had to love like love. 5. Out of the totality of: I came *from* a family full of women; I came *from* a family full of believers; I came *from* a pack of witches—I'm just waiting to conjure my powers; I came *from* a legacy of lovers— I'm just waiting to seduce my seducer; I came *from* a pride of proud women, and we take good care of our young. 6. As being other or another than: He couldn't tell me *from* his mother; he couldn't tell me *from* his sister; he couldn't tell me *from* the last woman he had before me, and why should he—we're all the same woman. 7. With (some person, place, or thing) as the instrument, maker, or source: Here's a note *from* my mother, and you can take it as advice *from* me: A weak lover is more dangerous than a strong enemy; if you're going to love someone, make sure you know where they're coming *from*. 8. Because of: Becoming an alcoholic, learning to walk away, being a good speller, being good in bed, falling in love—they all come *from* practice. 9. Outside or beyond the possibility of: In the room, he kept me *from* leaving by keeping me curious; he kept me *from* drowning by holding my breath in his mouth; yes, he kept me *from* leaving till the next day when he said *Leave*. Then, he couldn't keep me *from* coming back.

Wedding Night

John

let's strip off our words
to speak without our tongues. let's
try to tongue without
saying a word. let's turn speech
back into struggle tonight.

MacNolia

no, in the middle
of the night, afternoon, or
morning, let's pull up
our voice, our moan, yes, our song.
at 3:00 a.m. bring back words.

John

why bring words when we've
waited so long for silence?
why bring light when we've needed
to knead heat from our shadows?
when dark rooms call out our names?

MacNolia

in the shadow's heat,
in the dark's light, in the night's
promise of morning,
there's always a language born
out of the struggle to touch.

John

I don't know if I
have the words to touch the back
of your knees, the small
of your back . . . brown lines in your
palms . . . what language can frame you?

MacNolia

our language frames us
as we resemble our words.
the words we speak when
an open window carries
our new language to rooftops.

John

and here I thought I
was teaching you! now, you show
me a mirror in
which I see a stranger. how
good it is to meet *me* when—

MacNolia

when we are standing,
nose to nose, as my wedding
dress falls to our floor.

John

Looking for Work

I run like all the other men,
chasing my shadow down alleys.

I rub my hands over fire-mouthed barrels
instead of MacNolia's body, who still

stands tall and soft beneath her apron
and gloves, her housedress and rags.

I think about her leaving home in the numb air
Of morning to clean Dr. Wittenberg's home

for $5.00 a week. I see the other women,
in service, who came to Akron from turpentine

camps and cotton fields
to live out freedom songs—

songs to be lived not sung. At supper, what can
I say to her? What can I say?

I lick my hands. She looks at me.
I lower my eyes. I leave to meet

the other men. I wonder from where
the next meal will conjure.

So I leave home like a man who has a job
or one who used to and doesn't know

what else to do in a home but leave out
and move around like the snake's body

without the head but the haunting
memory of what his purpose is.

Red Ball Express

Just now a silence grows too loud to ignore
and I move out into the near-dark darkness,
which, these days, has become my daylight,
driving a 2.5 ton battalion truck to Red Ball depots
to pick up gasoline and ammunition, then,
ferrying them back to the 225th's positions
through land mines hiding beneath our wheels
and past German eyes, which illuminate the trees.
This is the hell I do, my mission brings
gasoline, which Clemenceau calls
"the red blood of war," *le sang rouge de guerre,*
like he's the one driving the gas-lit truck,
Churchill says the Allies *floated to victory*
on a sea of oil—on our flesh, he should say—
through backroads where enemy fire
shines like stars through black sky.
Let's face it, gentlemen, it's like General
Patton said, *My men can eat their belts,*
But my tanks gotta have gas.
Now, what keeps me going
is the precise shape of driver John Rookard
as he set out on a road to deliver supplies
the night after another driver had been ambushed
and killed—two tons of gasoline
as his funerary pyre—

it's Rookard's smile and his eyes,
which don't smile, as he turns and
is embraced by the darkness.
The shape of him behind the wheel,
burning in my eye,
is everything I need
to know about where I'm going.

Dr. Wittenberg

In Service

Akron, Ohio, 1948

All of our neighbors are jealous:
MacNolia, with a mop
Or broom, a washboard or iron,
Is a magician.
Come over next week and bring
Some laundry—we'll show you
What she can do. She can spell
Any word you can pretty much
Think of; although—at least,
I'm not sure—I don't believe
She knows what they all mean.
They say she almost went to college.
Would you believe she wanted
To be a surgeon?
(She told us when she interviewed
To work here.) How could we say no?
But—lucky for us, I guess—she
Didn't get a scholarship.
Maybe she's saving up for her son
To go; I'll have to remember to ask.
She stays over on North St.
In a little home with her husband,
Who has some kind of off-and-on
Job, and they seem to do pretty well

For themselves with what she makes
Working in service here.
They say she
Spelled like a demon as a child.
They say she was almost
The national spelling champ, would've
Been the second one we had
From Akron in as little as three years. . . .
I don't know, really, but I'm telling you—
She's the best damn maid in town.

after Marilyn Nelson

John Montiere *answer to question two*

Yellowed walls; hardwood floors injecting splinters when I walked barefoot; a torn lamp shade; a kitchen built for one butt to fit in; one bathroom, no shower; laundry hung on a line out back, smelling sweet; the funk of boiling cabbage on Mondays; the good funk of fish on Fridays; red velvet cake; pecan pie; "Bitch, I said come here" and "I saw you, I saw you" and "I said I ain't drunk"; how good I used to be at kickball, free frog, and tetherball; fireflies caught in a jar, glowing like a lantern; "Bitch, I oughta take a belt to your ass" and "Nigga, don't you know I'll kill you"; Papa peeing down from the top of the stairs—that's all I remember about my mama's house.

John

Jesse Owens, 1963

Football Hall of Fame Induction Ceremony
Canton, Ohio

He had aged and looked
Like a man at the end of a long

Race. And when I got close
To him, close enough to taste

His breath, his breath smelled
Like bourbon and I recoiled

From the picture in my mind
Of him sitting at the end

Of a bar, at the half
Light of his life.

I could not reach out to ask
For an autograph, but

I reached out to take his hand,
Just another baton exchange

Of the truths of life
As when you're old enough

To know what it smells like,
And you get scared

Because it smells familiar,
And you begin to tremble,

Seeing the runner
Before you, extending his hand,

Still panting.

Infidelity

Sometimes you learn words
By living them and sometimes
Words learn you

By defining who you are—
An eponym for appetite,
Lack of trust,

A volcano, a swash
Of lust and lies,
And here you come,

Introducing yourself
As John or some other
Alias defined by any

Trick your tongue
Can conjure, and,
Before you know

The meaning of the word,
Love has brought us
Back again and again.

There's always a cure
For love, but it hurts;

And, yes, there's always

A cure for the hurt,
But the remedy drags us
Right back

To where we started.

after William Matthews

John

When MacNolia Greases My Hair

Every drop of coconut oil
Is a kiss on my scalp;
Every twist of black strands,
An embrace; every groove parted
By her comb, a drawn curtain
Through which I invite her to walk;
Every struggle to untangle my coils,
A trill in a song from her voice;
And when the songs won't come,
We wrap our skins in silence,
And when the silence gets too loud,
We wrap ourselves in each other.

af · ter · glow \⇀\ *n.* 1. The light esp. in the Ohio sky after sun-
set: as in the look of the mother-of-pearl air during the morning's
afterglow. 2. The glow continuing after the disappearance of a
flame, as of a match or a lover, and sometimes regarded as a type
of phosphorescent ghost: This balm, this bath of light / This
cocktail of lust and sorrow, / This rumor of faithless love on a
neighbor's lips, / This Monday morning, this Friday night, / This
pendulum of my heart, / This salve for my soul, / This tremble
from your body / This breast aflame, this bed ablaze / Where you
rub oil on my feet, / Where we spoon and, before sunrise, turn
away / And I dream, eyes open, / swimming / In this room's pitch-
dark landscape.

John Montiere *answer to question three*

I see my son pulled from between MacNolia's legs. I see my son's legs kicking from between her legs. Blood paints the skin of the midwife's hands and arms up to her elbows. Blood paints my son's legs up to his waist; all I can see is his kicking. He is grounded, feet first. His head emerges and he sings his song. His voice is like a gust of wind throwing a man's head back or, like a wind whispering through a woman's hair. He cannot open his eyes. He squints hard for his song is passionate. What I can see of his eyes are slits of coal. His skin thins so I can see the workings of his body: blood runs from his fingers to his toes, spreads veins like branches palming his scalp, pin-stripes his arms. He is covered in blood.

with (=) *prep.* 1. against: It started in the fall of 1950, a fight *with* my husband John. He could not accept my being pregnant. But, as I told him, he didn't have a problem when we were conceiving it. 2. from: It was like parting *with* a friend, being pregnant. John became distant: distant lying next to me in bed, distant inside me in bed, distant walking out the door in the morning. 3. in mutual relation to: He talked *with* my brother, who had always been a friend to John. On that day, they were just two men talking. Brother's language was plain. "You do good by my sister." After that, we changed the way we talked *with* each other. 4. in the company of: The next Friday, I went to the movies *with* him. He helped me climb the steps to the balcony, that nigger heaven, which I didn't feel like climbing to; I was as big as the movie house itself, eight months' pregnant. He held my hand in the dark, fed me popcorn. He held my hand all the way home, and I knew again why I was *with* him. 5. As regards, toward: John is not a patient man. And I wondered: could he show patience *with* children? 6. In support of: I wanted to hear him say he was *with* me, even when I looked one pillow down and saw him lying next to me. For once, I needed to hear a man say what his actions were already telling me: he was *with* me and he wasn't going to leave. 7. in the presence of or containing: I needed to know we were like Lipton tea *with* sugar: better together than apart. 8. in the opinion of or as judged by: I couldn't take it if we had another argument, not in my ninth month; these moments had weight *with* me. 9. Because of, through: I could tell John was going to be blue *with* pride, especially if we had a boy—as if this were all his doing. And I'd be happy *with* that. 10. Despite: Even *with* all his earlier protests, he kept a smile on his face when our son, Darrell, was born. 11. given, granted: *With* his blessing, we baptized our son, and they both cried, both like grown men, for a man never changes the way he cries, always as if he were the coming of spring.

Darrell Cox, John and MacNolia's son

"One Bourbon, One Scotch, One Beer"

The Silver Leaf Lounge on Howard Street, Akron

Brer Andrew moves through his joint
Making peace among strangers:
He'd water down the drinks, but what's the point?

Tonight, the crowd is eager
To toast a couple's silver endurance.
There's a man who has never

Been drunk, and he hasn't
Seen his woman in over a week.
He orders his drinks, losing patience,

Three at a time. And at their peak,
Two piano players get their left hands goin';
Getting people out their seats,

Their right hands are filled with progressions,
Cuttin' each other down.
'Drew dances with his wife, flirtin',

Or makes it work with his wooden leg, alone.
Eardrums beat like a rhythm section.
A silver voice brushes over the microphone;

Fingers stride over piano keys—the friction
Of 88 gapped teeth grinnin' without love—
Bringin' the crowd to their feet and to confusion

'Cause now the crowd wants blood,
'Cause now the crowd wants laughter
And people start to shove

As Brer Andrew escorts Mr.
Three-at-a-time—holding him by the elbow,
With another grip on his neck—out the door.

That was one bad boy,
Drew says, *They tell me a woman shot*
His nuts off up in Chicago.

Elegy to My Son

February 18, 1970. The city is more overcast
Than ever. My shadow gains
Weight beneath my steps
As we slow drag out the front door.
The trombones of your life, in their deepest
Tones, are playing a dirge.
When I want to laugh, I feel your presence and miss
Your presence; whenever I see something beautiful
I wait to hear you say, *Now, ain't that somethin'*,
The way you used to say, *Ain't this* or *that* something
Whenever some car, or flower, or suit, or gesture
Was worthy of your eye.

January 12, 1970. Twilight dims.
You're driving your father's car on I-76,
The driver of the other car already drunk,
Maybe heartbroken, maybe unemployed,
Or living in his backseat—
I don't know. I don't even care—
The trombones are stretching to their full length.

January 11, 1970. You said you had
To take care of a little business.
No doubt your hand was around some woman's waist,
Your face in her hair, a drumbeat in your bones,
As you sipped pinot noir for the first time, and whispered

To her—how brown the lines shimmered in her palm;
How brown, under cocoa butter, her shoulders,
Her back and thighs.
You thought the war had ended
In afterglow, in sepia-toned memories,
In letters sent thousands of miles in your hand-
Writing to her hands. The trombones were muted, adagio.

December 15, 1969. We cannot wait
For your return home. Your father is changing
The oil in the car so you'll have a way
To get around town. For once, we'll share
A car, like we had to when we only had one.
Your coming home has already brought us closer.

September 12, 1950. Trombones blaring.
And your father and I are reborn in the bronze
Discs of your eyes. For a few moments,
We're all glimmers of laughter, as if twilight
Were a constant and the glow of your fingers
And toes, your bright cry, your sequined
Heartbeat, all were a new grammar
For us to say the most complicated
Truths in the simplest way.

November 3, 1969. Nixon announces 60,000 men
Will return home; you are one of them. All is awaiting
You: your father and me, your girlfriend, her cocoa skin,
The bottle of wine, your father's car. . . .

John

I'm Trying

To blind you to my sins,
I'm trying to unbutton my shirt
To let the light pour out;
I'm trying to walk you across
The terrain of my body.
The affair I had with the woman
I saw downtown crossing the street
As she rushed off on the horizon.
The touch I cherished like a man on parole
From the clerk handing me chance
In the form of nickels and dimes.
I'm trying to find what I need between
The twisted sheets on our bed.
I'm trying to admit I cry when the underdog
Wipes the sand from his cheeks.
I'm trying to speak
To you about the fears ticking
In my ribcage.

The woman walking with a broken heel.
The man boasting while tomato soup stains his tie.
The child crawling with a full diaper. I'm trying
To conceal my faults and learn from them.
I'm trying to apologize for my life
Before I met you and my father's example.
I'm trying to hush

The voice of the ghost of past lovers
Who has no mercy.

I'm not trying to run
From the smile creased
In the arch of your foot.
I'm not trying to find
Any more words to say
It's your voice, your voice, your voice. . . .

A woman carries a bag of laundry
As large as a mouth full of lies.
A man strikes a hammer upon an anvil
With the same care he uses to lift
A child over his head.
Listen, I'm trying to be the stone
You wield to slay the giant or
To skip across a pond.

Dust

Off the lamp shade

         so we can see

              each other

    without/groping,

without

    the mystery,

        the fantasy,

of who we wish we were;

        dust

off the piano so

      we can dance

   weightless

like grace

    notes

    under Art Tatum's

fingers, dust

---

off the television so we can
settle on the sofa till our bodies
feel like the letter **B**,

---

till our minds

    misplace

        regrets,

   till our tongues become extinct.

Lift   the   dust
off   your   eyes,
girl;

lift   the   velvet   haze
off   your   dreams;   wipe
the   surface
clean;   t e a r
the   rag   off   your   head,   and

peer   *Ard I walked out one evening?*

before

there's nothing left to see.

MacNolia

Scenes from My Scrapbook

Entry: Akron, Ohio, April 22, 1936

"I'm glad I won, and I hope I win in Washington."
> MacNolia Cox, age 13,
>> after winning the Akron District Spelling Bee

With braces on his legs, FDR wins by a landslide, and split-
ting atoms is just a mad scientist's theory and although civil
rights is no more than a subplot in science fiction, I just won
the city-wide spelling bee, ten years after four Klansmen
were elected to the school board, and I'm going to the Palace
Theatre in Cleveland as the special guest of Fats Waller
and Bill "Bojangles" Robinson. I can spell like they can
sing and dance. I've never seen so many white people
smile at me; I've never seen so many white people afraid.
I can spell every thing I can read. 100,000 words, baby,
right here in my head. I might be a doctor or a lawyer
or I might just spell for a living. I'm the first,
but all I can do is spell what I know.
I'm the first black to win, whatever that means.

Later, America no longer elects presidents with disabilities,
the atomic bomb has conquered mankind, and we've assassinated
all the fallen angels. All but me, I'm just not spelling,
I'm cleaning. It's hard to spell with a child straddled on your hip,
with the country at war, with food that's got to find its way
to the table. I've got a good man, but he can't do it on his own.
These are hard times for the white man, can you imagine

what it's like for mine? It's harder now for him than it was for me
when I went to Washington. I spelled those white kids into tears.
I could spell whatever they threw at me: *felicitation*—
    f-e-l-i-c-i-t-a-t-i-o-n,
which is what I got. *Apoplexy*—A-p-o-p-l-e-x-y, which is what
    they had
when I got into the final five. But they would have that no more
than they would have me to win. They pulled a word not on
    the list,
the goddess of vengeance: *Nemesis*—N-e-m-e-s-i-s—I couldn't
    spell it, then.

But for now, say it's spring in Akron, Ohio; the smokestacks
smudge the skyline even at dusk when the sun paints pastels. I
    read
the dictionary starting with the *A*'s and keep on going.
I spell even when they tell me to sit in the colored section,
even when they don't give scholarships to colored girls for college.
I spell the names of the dead who came before my name.
Before me, what I do had only been a prayer on a black girl's
    tongue.
What more can I ask for? There's a revolution wetting my lips.
I'm 13 years old, I can spell, and I'm black. All
odds are against me, but all my people are counting on me.
I've already done what had not been done before. What
complaint should I file? My spelling has cast a spell
on this country. All the signs glower *White Only,* but I keep
    spelling
and I'm twice as good as a Negro girl has any right to claim.

MacNolia

This Life

"Say *this life* and let it be enough, for once."

Joe Bolton
American Variations

If you say *obscenity*, o-b-s-c-e-n-i-t-y
It doesn't sound like a bad word;
It sounds like the name of a child
On her mother's lips; it sounds like my name

When slid from my mother's tongue.
My pulse would shift into place
As her voice traveled through my veins.
Say MacNolia—M-a-c-N-o-l-i-a—

And let my name bless the one who named me.
I'd pronounce my name and people would
Mistake it for a flower. Can you imagine me
Correcting white adults? *I said*

MAC-nolia. . . . No, I mean it was 1936—
It wasn't safe to spell my own name.
If you whispered it, a thought cloud
Grew over your head with the name, a colon

And the definition: a Negro who spells
And reads as well as [if not better than] any white.

Say *summer rain running over a brown girl's face,*
And you cannot mistake it for tears;

The syllables are as gentle as *summer*
Rain running over a brown girl's face.
Even at 13, I knew right from wrong:
Adam bit the apple and we all could see.

Say *truth* and let it be true, for once.
Watch the mouth take a bite;
Let the juice run over the lips;
Let the tongue know the taste.

If I had one breath of advice to give
To myself at 13, some language
That would have helped me understand
The grammar of my life, I would have said

What I still know: Girl, savor what you learn
And spit it back as best you know how.

The Night Richard Pryor Met Mudbone

"It is spiritless to think you cannot attain to that which you have seen
and heard the masters attain. The masters are men. You are also a man."

Yamamoto Tsunetomo

Hagakure: The Book of the Samurai

The moon hung orange as any sun
Just before it faces evening,
Like a flaming breast in the sky
Calling my name, and I walked out

Under it and rubbed the moonlight
All over my face and hands the way
The old folks used to do with sunlight
On Wednesdays, because, back in those times—

The hard times, harder than any of this shit
We're faced with today—they said, *The only*
Time the sun came out was on Wednesdays—
If you were lucky—and a boy had to get

His ass up early just to catch that. Well,
It was a day like that that I'm about to tell you
About, a day when all I could see were
The mismatched symbols on the slot machine

Of my life. Surprisingly, this isn't a story
About a woman. All my relationships with women
Were one long-legged story in high heels.
But I'm not even trying

To get to sex here, for once.
What I'm trying to say is when your foot
Brushes a woman's toes under the sheets,
When you feel her breath on the back of your neck,

Turning your spine into a tall building,
When your eyes meet hers while making love,
You know you're looking at the truth.
The truth is what I found whenever I thought life

Could prove better than the craps game I was born into,
Although it's always just a roll of the dice;
Like that time in Vegas when I walked out
On stage—half-high, half-drunk—

In 1968, and there sat Dean Martin in the front row,
Drink in one hand and a half-burned out cigarette
In his other cuff-linked hand, and I looked at his
Seal-hide hair and his wax-figure of a face,

And the rest of the audience went out of focus,
All the voices were put on mute; all I could hear was
Dino stirring the ice in his drink and I asked myself
What the fuck am I doing here, my skinny, black

Ass from Peoria, Illinois? I walked out on stage and a switch
Flipped off inside my head. The room went white.
My agent told me—like in the movies, man,
Told me on the phone real chill like—he said I'd never work

In this life again. But then I realized
It wasn't neon marquees, gangsters
Or headline acts I was afraid of—it was me.
I spent years imitating Bill Cosby, telling jokes

That fit me like a suit two sizes too big;
I struck a sad figure on stage, even when I was good.
Don Rickles came up to me once and said,
What a great show! It's amazing how much you sound

Like Cosby. And then I wondered if everyone else could
Tell I had climbed inside his skin and zipped him up;
I wondered who else would unzip my monologue
And find me there trembling.

After Vegas I headed to New York and got to open
For Miles Davis at the Village Gate, and Miles
Looked through me just like Rickles had, but he did
Something that was as beautiful as his music:

Miles knew I was looking for a way
To fall off the planet's edge, gettin' high and wanting more,
So one night as I sat drinking in my dressing room, the
Emcee comes in right before curtain and tells me

Miles changed the lineup. I thought I was fired, man.
But Miles decided that he was going to open for *me*.

Do you know what a bad muthafucka you gotta be
To have Miles Davis open for you? That's like God, Jack.

So I go out on stage, and as I'm about to go into my best
Bill Cosby impression, I see this old man with coal-
Colored skin sitting on the edge of the stage.
He's lookin' at me like, *Well, boy, let's see what*

You've got. And I don't want to hear none of that Bill Cosby shit,
Either. And he said tell them about badass Oilwell; about the
    Wino;
Or about Miss Rudolph, the Hoodoo lady, *How she had one titty*
That had an eye tattooed on it and 'nother that had

A mouth, and how when that one titty blew a kiss
And the other winked, you knew, for the first time,
You had smoked enough of that shit.
I asked the old man his name and he said

They call me Mudbone; I was born in Tupelo, Mississippi.
I looked at him sideways, and he said, *That's a city, boy.*
I was born there long time ago. So long ago it ain't worth
Rememberin' when exactly, because after a certain while,

It's just a long time ago.
Like me, I could tell he died
Many times and had some stories to tell;
You don't live this long being a fool.

There's a whole lot of wise, young men
Deader than a muthafucka, he said.
Yes, I thought, my meditations on Death keep me alive,
Too; Death would show up, from time to time,

Like a distant relative
Who thought I had been away too long.
The funny thing is, I spent years searching—
Laughing on the tip of a needle,

Crying between a woman's legs, imitating
Other people's work—just to come
Back to a man who had been there all along saying,
Hey, look over here at me, but I had ignored him

Thinking he didn't have anything to say.
So I stood there with a cigarette throbbing in one hand
And a microphone rocking in the other
And I told them about the fallen angels of my life.

And I grabbed a handful of the glow from the spotlights,
Rubbed it all over my body, right on stage, naked,
In front of everybody, and I smiled, and they smiled back,
As the light, growing brighter now from the rafters,

Turned to sunshine.

John, 1976

Death Letter Blues Ghazal

You deserve to read the books in heaven.
The pages deserve your hands in heaven.

Baby, you deserve to read and drink well.
The pages desire your hands in heaven.

An anklet and a ring adorn your feet;
Now, let's see you do your dance in heaven.

⌐⌐

Storefront mannequins are sad in small towns.
They look like souls put on hold for heaven.

Say, storefront mannequins pose in small towns
Like souls on line at the gates of heaven.

Grab a mink coat for your shoulders, baby,
Drag it behind, as you walk in heaven.

⌐⌐

I got word from a friend; you won't be home.
It's a long track to those gates in heaven.

I got the bad word; you ain't comin' home.
It's a long track to the gates in heaven.

I can still see you playing with your hair . . .
Is this for me my last piece of heaven?

In my dream, you have a mole—cheek, breast, leg;
It rolls over your body in heaven.

In my dream, I am your mole—leg, breast, cheek;
I roll over your body in heaven.

Curve of your back, open mouth, scarf in hair—
With eyes closed, John still sees you in Heaven.

John, 1980

Unforgettable

*INTERIOR—DAY—JOHN sits at the edge of his bed in his
room, which has become stark and dingy over the past four years.
Sunlight outlines the window; the shade is pulled down. A raw
lightbulb swings from the ceiling. The camera should be hand
held. A boom mic hangs overhead. JOHN speaks:*

(Medium One Shot.)

JOHN

Although MacNolia knew about the other women,
She buried her heart in the sand

As if cheating never happened.
Now she's gone and it's like my lies hang upside down

In this room and when I turn off the lights,
Just as I think I'm finding peace, they play in the dark.

But, you know, the truth was also kisses on her shoulders
In the middle of the night. The other women

Were like some dream for me,
A nightmare for her.

Dangerous thing, when a poor man dreams.
It feels like a shoeshine man

Eyeballin' a strand of pearls in a storefront
Window, wishing he could buy it with tips,

But you know how the story ends:
All he can do is walk away, backwards,

With his heart rattling
In his chest like loose change.

This is how it went down when we went to see
Nat King Cole at the Palace Theater. I remember

After his show we saw Nat stroll
Into the Silver Leaf Lounge

With his wife. Now, I'm telling you this: Mac didn't know
It then, but I was already unemployed. And here I was, broke,

With my wife, worrying about him: wondering how gravity
Keeps a man on the ground, while everyone lifts him up.

(*Extreme Close-Up of JOHN's Mouth*)

When everyone knows the gates of heaven
Are your lips parting open with song, what keeps you

From blotting out the sun? When you have so much power
And someone spits on you, tells you *you're too black,*

How do you remember to smile?
(Pull back to Medium shot) I looked at Nat

And wondered about Mr. Love
And Mr. Hate wrestling in his chest and wondered if

Love's arms could really be so strong. Or was Nat
In so much pain his swallow looked like a smile?

And then I looked at MacNolia and wished
I could be the silver-voiced one, but I never got the tone

Right, the gesture, the way Nat lit his wife's cigarette,
Or brushed crumbs from her cheek.

I didn't want Nat's wife or to take anything
From him, I just wanted *Mac* to hear the music

His wife heard when nothing was said, when they just looked
Into each other's eyes. All he had to do was look at her

And she heard "Unforgettable" over and over again.
And when we went home, I played their song for us

And we danced, and I pretended I had his creamy voice
And his vinyl hair. But when she looked at me, man,

She looked scared, like I had her in the air
And she thought I'd drop her. And so I tried to smile

Like Nat, but I knew she had good reason
To keep her eyes on the ground.

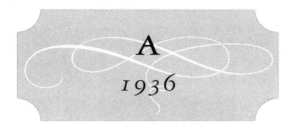

A
1936

"A brake is applied to the action, and the tension is
screwed tighter."

Sergei Eisenstein
"The Unexpected"
Film Form: Essays in Film Theory

MacNolia, 13 years old

English

Everything I know has just come to me.
For instance, I know the moon smiling

Over the eastside of Akron
Is also over Havana, maybe with a gold tooth.

I know our next-door neighbor is crying
Because she now knows about her husband's

Girlfriend and something hurtful was said.
I know without a bell, an alarm clock

Screams as quietly as a woman too afraid to scream.
I know, after a month of Nadinola, I cannot change

My skin, and I know it's a lie: lye
Will *(not)* straighten kinky hair. It makes you bald.

I learned the word *chiaroscuro*
By rolling it on my tongue

Like cotton candy the color
Of day and night.

On the radio,
I heard Orson Welles

Say *Let's surge ahead,*
And blood rushed up

My legs like a bad boy's eyes.
And I kept saying

Surge . . . surge . . . in a whisper,
Pursing my lips

As if I were about to taste
My first kiss.

⁓

Walking past the State Store,
An already drunk man

Fixed his mouth to say,
In a slurred British accent,

Mmm, don't you look fetching,
And I felt like running

After a stick
To catch it in my teeth,

Just to bury it
In the creases of his face.

A boy who has hands as big
As my father's, makes me

Think of *honeydew*
Whenever he waves Hello

Because I once saw him pinch a honeybee
To death right in the mouth of a tulip.

Wow, we said, *he's just **like** a man.*
And I remember asking Josephine,

Who is 18 and knows everything,
What was he wiping on his shirt,

And she said it was like what she was
Eating, which was a honeydew melon.

She shoved it in my face. It was sweet
And cold in my mouth.

And when I say it, *ho-ney-dew*,
I always have to lick my lips.

On page 981 of *Webster's* dictionary,
In the *F*s, the first word on the page is *fondle.*

The last word on the page is *foot.*
Neither word is hard to spell.

Neither word strikes me
By itself, but the two words

Next to each other in the upper
Right-hand margin leads me to the *J*s

To find *juxtapose*, which carries the weight
Of couples, who, my mom says, realize they're

Better together than they were
Before they met, which she says,

With growth and time, after I finish
School, I'll understand,

But which also makes my journey to the *Z*s
As contorted as the letter itself.

Life only seems clear
Through the words I trade

With others. It's not the same
As the tongue I use

When talking to myself.
As when from somewhere

In the dark waters of my chest
The diaphragm contracts—

Just a gentle squeeze, really—
As I look a boy in the eye,

Or not, and reach
For his face, if I dare.

after Tim Seibles

to (רל) *prep.* **1a.** In a direction toward so as to reach: As in, when we went *to* the picnic, I saw how the men didn't look at you, how when they walked *to* you, it was only because you were in my orbit, how when you walked *to* the table where they drank and sang and licked their fingers of food, you didn't look at them either, how when you skipped over *to* the lot where the boys played, they simply played and you played with them till it got dark and then you simply stopped playing, without my saying a word, which made me smile. **b.** Toward: And you turned *to* me, and I told you the heavy truth: you'll get through this life on your spelling, not your smile; on your math, not your legs; on the many sciences of life, not your sex. And this, my dear, is when you were born a woman. **2a.** Reaching as far as: Then I didn't feel like a mother. I looked into your eyes; water was clear *to* the bottom, the loose steel that hardens us from girlhood through womanhood was already damn near *to* the base of your skull. **b.** To the extent or degree of: I loved your father *to* distraction, which drove me *to* grief, which, I guess, drove him *to* a younger woman, who hadn't yet learned this much about men. Which is why I tell you now, I love you. I love you all the way *to* your next life, which should get you, at least, halfway, through this one. **c.** With the resultant condition of: When you were born, the first time, you came early and weak and near dead and I prayed you back *to* life. **3.** Toward a given state: Your hair in a ponytail, the white satin strap of your slip slung over your brown shoulder, the crescent moon of your foot from which a red shoe dangles in mid-July— girl, none of these will help women *to* equality. **4.** In contact with; against: When the Ohio snow came *to* our eyes, when the sun came *to* the eastside steaming off the sidewalks, when the leaves came *to* the ground, when your father left, before we tired of waiting, we pressed our faces *to* the windows. 5. Opposite; near or in front of: And when I finally saw you chest *to* chest with a boy, I reminded you of the year of your father's leaving. I held you *to* my breast. I warned you: don't place a great deal of importance on holding a man close *to* your heart. 6. Used to indicate appropriation or possession of or belonging with: Being a wife *to* a man is like being a lid *to* a jar: if she doesn't open, he tries warming her up, loosening her grip, and if she doesn't fit, he'll simply try another lid. 7. Concerning; regarding: As *to* your father, after many years had passed, after your winning the local spelling bee, after your picture appeared on the front page of the paper, after you were a finalist in the national competition, after we came back and the city threw a parade in your honor downtown, did I tell you, I never gave an answer *to* any of his letters? Never. 8. Used before a verb to indicate the infinitive: There are women who will never get *to* know their fathers and won't get over it. There are women who have had *to* know their fathers and won't get over it. There are women who know what it is *to* live with a man, but who will never know what it is *to* marry a man; and there are women who know what it is *to* marry a man, but who will never know what it is *to* live.

Mrs. Alberta Cox

Rope

As if two girls were starting a fire
On all sides of my daughter,
She is set ablaze: the girls swing
Two clotheslines between them
As if they were goddesses
Holding two country roads
Leading to each other; neighbors
Surround her syncopated dance
As her seizure of heat begins
To flicker on the moonlit sidewalk—
Now, the ropes are white hot—
Her hair ignites in the upswing; her barrettes,
Like petrified butterflies, click on the off beat;
Her knees pump like she's walking on red coals;
Her arms flail as if she's calling the rain
To put her out; she jumps, she flirts
With the flame: she jumps backwards
And then turns forward,
Rocking in and out of the light,
Her hands testify around her head
Or pose on yet-to-be hips, till
Her fire snuffs out as a wind blows cold,
A car with flashing lights
Slows past, and the braids of our summer night
Surrender to gravity.

Time Reviews The Ziegfeld Follies Featuring Josephine Baker, 1936

TIME REVIEW:

Before, we pictured her without *diamonds*,
Without sequined gowns and a face of *paint*.
We could see that this show was not the *time*
For a lithe St. Louis girl of her *race*
To flaunt her flanks in front of New York *men*.
How could she expect us to find *applause*,

When we had saved to throw coins of *applause*
To Fanny Brice[1], our star, a *diamond*
On a stage of lights? Besides, what these *men*
Wanted was a dream well drawn behind *paint*,
Not a life-size black doll flaunting her *race*
And wares as if this were her place and *time*.

Parisian and brown? This was not the *time*
For a poor Negro girl to find *applause*
When she had given up her one true *race*—
America—for filthy France. *Diamonds*
Draped from her neck and ears, but even *paint*
Chips on the wrong surface. A street *woman*

1. Fanny Brice, the longtime star of the Ziegfeld Follies,
was known for her talents as a comedienne as well as a singer.

Posing as a lady—please. Petty *men*
Could appreciate her dance, which was *timed*
To a beat of rags and old iron. *Paint*
The picture true, and let's save the *applause*
For patriots—Eve Arden, a *diamond,*
And Bob Hope, a charm—not this girl with *race*

On her hips and tongue. The spice of *race*
Can be sweet or tart; the lips of the *man*
Who tastes will be surprised. To think *diamonds*
Will clear the palate is a waste of *time.*
Sure, we gave *Princess Tam Tam*² an *applause,*
Even if she mumbled through songs and *paint,*

Even when she would cry and run her *paint,*
We listened. This is not about her *race*
But her choice of song, her need for *applause*
That would outshine Fanny Brice. Any *man*
Would give her a break, but the place and *time*
Was not this night. Yes, Brice was our *diamond.*

JOSEPHINE BAKER RESPONDS:

They want bananas on hips, not *diamonds*
On my décolletage. I'm under the *paint,*
Sinews dancing through segregated *time;*

2. *Princess Tam Tam* was a film starring Josephine Baker,
produced in 1935.

It's not all about jazz or even *race.*
Fanny Brice's bland version of "My Man,"[3]
In smoke-filled bars couldn't steal an *applause,*

So how do they think she deserves *applause*
On Broadway under lights and with *diamonds*
Dangling from her dewlap? I got a *man,*
He stays with me when I take off the *paint,*
And he doesn't care about this whole *race*
Hoopla; he loves Josephine for me. *Time*

Magazine just started taking the *time*
To acknowledge Negroes, and now *applause*
From them is supposed to predict *racial*
Equality on stage? Talent? *Diamonds*
Determine my success. They can go *paint*
Broadway as white as they please, all the *men*

On the *Champs* will tell you I'm the *woman*
By which they measure others; only *Time*
Had a problem with my act, when the *paint*
Comes off, that's all it comes down to: *applause*
From friends not foes. Just look at this *diamond*
On my hand from my Pepito[4]; does *race*

3. "My Man" was a popular song written by Maurice Yvain as "Mon Homme."
Later, the English lyrics were written by Channing Pollock for the
Ziegfeld Follies.
4. Pepito was Josephine Baker's fiancé from 1935–1936. He died of cancer
before she completed the run of the Ziegfeld Follies.

Refract in its eye, or light? You see *race*
Is not real, only light and love; no *man*,
Negro or white, can change that. The *diamond*
Holds so much truth because it endures *time*;
It struggles through nothingness for *applause*;
It holds its breath, dark, naked without *paint*

Or the benefit of believing *paint*
Will change things because she is the same *race*
As coal underneath it all. And *applause*
Is just some dream. At times, even my *man*
Who, after all, is white, doesn't see *time*
And again how I'm merely a *diamond*

Trying to catch some light under the *paint. Man*,
I'm telling you, *race* problems will change with *time*,
Long after *applause* and this *diamond*'s light fades.

Mrs. Alberta Cox

Morena

Deep in my pores
Lies the secret
Evidence of faith,

A black-licorice world
Beneath these everyday clothes,
Where men walk in silence

With dilated mouths.
Have you ever fallen
Into the vowels on a dark

Woman's lips as she blew
A simple phrase like *Good Morning*
To a man she's just met?

Nothing, maybe, to the naked ear,
But close your eyes and listen
To the dark sounds rounded

Off in the shadows of her mouth—
There lies the secret to end
All wars. In her throat,

Lives a lump of coal, which does not aspire
To emerge as a diamond. I know how
Her darkness, how her dark wake,

Sways in inverse light behind a man's
Eyelids as he reaches his hand
Toward the hint of her body.

Asa Philip Randolph

(Recruitment speech, 1936)

When a man wants to talk about love
But he can't because there's so much hate
Around him, when he realizes life
Is a ride meant for two, but people—
And, I want to be clear, white people
And some Negroes alike—want to make life
A fight built on a foundation of hate
And turmoil, it's hard to even think about love

Let alone talk about children and futures.
My own people, and I mean educated men
And women, would rather clean out
Spittoons than challenge the unions,
The president, the store clerk. Unions,
By their very name, say *Don't count me out!*
Yet, we don't see how strong a man's
Spirit must be to keep our eyes on the future

And not on a gun or a knife or any route
For which the flesh sincerely thirsts.
We should fight—not, mind you, to pretend
We're gods or act like our oppressors—
But by saying we're immune to oppression
And we want what is ours, by not pretending

We're silhouettes who pour when you're thirsty,
Who bow when you call, *Boy!* No, the route

I propose will not only place the Brotherhood
Of Sleeping Car Porters and Maids on equal
Terms with their white brothers and sisters,
But also put us on better terms with our own spirits.
Now, I know what you're thinking: *He's talking Spirit;*
Brother Randolph wants to preach. Brothers, sisters,
no. I listen; believe me. I can't talk equal
and speak down from the clouds. *Brotherhood,*

Sisterhood, equality, union, spirit—these are mere words.
Let me make it real for you: not too long ago, a man,
One of our own brothers among many, was on a train
Out of Chicago, when it, somehow, derailed
And burst into flames. And we were all derailed
By this event; there were no survivors. But on this train,
Among the wreckage, among the many bodies, was a man's
Unidentified body; around his neck were the words

Phi Beta Kappa, on a key he earned while a student
At Dartmouth College. Yet, he had no choice but to work
As a porter. There's nothing wrong with the job. Nothing.
But something's wrong—wrong with this country—when
He has no other choice but a job his father had when
School was not an option—his father, seen as nothing
But a boy in the eyes of men. Many of you today work
With hope smuggled under hats to see your kids as students

At some college someday. Do you want them to finish college
And work under similar conditions? Even if they choose
To dig ditches, shouldn't they, at least, be respected
Enough to be seen as *men* digging? I'm not trying to start
Any trouble, but I do want to be clear: I *am* trying to start
A charter under the AF of L and a contract, one that's respected,
With the Pullman Company. But we have to choose
First to see *ourselves* as viable workers, whether college

Educated or not; and, between you and me,
We have to loosen the tight reigns
Of the AF of L. It's been 12-years on our shoulders.
   Those train wheels be callin' till the stars break down
   Train wheels be callin' till the stars break down
   I got a rainbow wrapped around my shoulder
   It ain't gonna rain, Lawd, Lawd, it ain't gonna rain.
So come on, people; stand on your feet! Walk with me.

after Edward Hirsch

Green Pastures

Negroes stretched out on chaise-lounge clouds. Negroes in togas suspended by wires. An old, Negro man with wings bigger than a railroad worker's hands. Negroes in a letter-boxed, black and white heaven. Although the scene includes a group of girls screaming through double-Dutch rope, ice-cream trucks ringing through the neighborhood with Technicolor flavors—after all, we all dream color when we're watching black and white—this is heaven and all the joys of life are provided without the guilt. All the joys of life are provided without the fears. The joys of laughter. The joys of forgetting.

The Sunday school class fills with folk tales and gospel, a light streams from Mr. Deshee's Good Book, and Negro girls dream of Negro girls in the hereafter hula-hooping with halos.

And, on screen, it's true: in the by and by, the movie house lines sprawl around the block; the balcony opens only by choice; Jim Crow works on the long track in hell; and every water fountain wears a sign, *Negroes, Too*, as elegantly as a middle-aged woman wears a strand of pearls.

Practice

You know how a word comes
To you like a face that's familiar
But without a name to which you can
Attach—not a complete stranger,
But not a friend either?

You stare into the features of this word,
Hoping the letters will find you—
You know they will find you;
You repeat the word to yourself
As if tasting it will help.

Mother looks at the word
On the index card—
Not at me, but the word—
Nodding her head as if my repeating it
Were an answer; she hangs on to my voice,

Trying to reassure me, but her eyes
Are not convinced. This makes me nervous.
I begin writing the word in the sweat
Of my left palm with my right index finger.
I repeat the word again, louder,

As if I have a receipt for it in my pocket:
IRIDESCENT, I-RI-DE-SCENT.
And the question of origin comes to mind.
So I ask: *What's the origin?*
She reads: *formed from Latin,* iridis,
        rainbow, 1796

What's the definition?
You don't know this one? She asks.
The judges aren't going to ask that;
They're going to give me the definition, Ma.
Sigh. She reads from the dictionary:

iridescent: *adj.* 1. Producing a display of lustrous rainbow like
colors. 2. brilliant, lustrous, or colorful in effect or appearance.

I feel sorry for those of you
Who don't know moments like this:
My palms dry. We watch ten letters
Lift off the page and spill
From my mouth like a magician pulls

A prism of scarves from his ear:
i-r-i-d-e-s-c-e-n-t. I watch the light catch
The brown of her eyes. I ask if I'm right.
Is that it? I say, *I wasn't sure*
If it had two Rs or just one.

She pauses for a second, still
Looking down at the word.
Yeah, baby, each word just like that.
I nod my head. She's still looking down
As if afraid for herself.

I realize nothing I spell sounds true.
Every round will be like the first time.
The light has run from her eyes.
She's quiet again.
Next word, I say.

Akron Spelling Bee, April 22, 1936

The Akron Armory

Maxine Schumate, Round 24

1.

As far as I've come, there is no turning back;
There is no light brighter than this win,
This long-awaited stage, universe of eyes
In the dark, flashbulbs, whispers, heartbeats, and—
Not without trying, but through my own labor—
This all falls at a point near my feet, at the edge
Of the stage, a whole armory of bodies balance
On every word I spit out; hell, every letter and they
Want more, more, 24 rounds is not enough,
But I can't believe I've already spelled through more
Rounds than Tunney survived when he fought Dempsey.
I've had people ask for my picture, my autograph
And I've been in the paper and I'm not even 16 yet. . . .

2.

You hear me? In the paper and not even 16 yet—
How many people can say they've done what their
Folks could only dream of doing. That's what these

Lights and cameras and 0-shaped mouths
Are all about: doing what others may never
Do. How many people can hush an audience
With one letter uttered from their mouth?
How many of you will know a love this fragile,
This immense, this short-lived and passionate?
This is the big tent of words and the final
Round could make any one of us the ringmaster.
Each word, each syllable measured and dissected,
Each breath held and exhaled holds the present and
Future history hostage at the knife point of my tongue.

John Huddleston, Round 35

1.

The crowd has come to see our minds contort
Sounds into syllables, syllables into letters
And all without the benefit of meaning;
You know, no one cares what the words
Mean, just the spelling, for which I am thankful.
Lord, what could bring more pressure?
It's not like I mind losing to a girl, but a Negro . . .
I've been told that I can't lose to a Negro;
No one ever has. Now I know how the pressure
Of competition raises the blood. I am thankful
This is the final round; these spotlights hang like swords.
One day I'll wonder: what was the meaning

Of all this? When will I stop mouthing letters
Before I sleep? God, when will her brown lips contort?

2.

I came to win; I don't have many choices.
I came to make my mama proud—
A boy, my age, my height—which is not easy
Growing as fast as teeth in a child's mouth
Or disappointment in a parent's heart. I'm awkward;
I'm not so good at basketball, or baseball
But I complete a Dalí painting when I spell.
I speak and the crowd falls under the spell
Of words like stars hung on wire in this dark ball-
Room, or gymnasium, or class; all the awkward
Dances of my life stop in my mouth.
They listen in disbelief at the impossible made easy.
It's a waltz through the pages of a dictionary, and I'm proud
To live this dream for those who don't have this choice.

MacNolia Cox, Round 36

1.

Not the cast and measure of words
Out of the announcer's mouth—
After all, he simply reads them—
But watching phonics land

In John Huddleston's frontal lobe,
His six foot, two inch, 14-year-old
Body; the balance of his spirit
And his flesh, an inflection of the future,
A playground of all possibility . . .
Mortal. He's blushing; he's sweating.
And I love him for it: the weight
We all carry, the weight I clench between
   My teeth, suppress under my tongue.
   Each syllable rings like notes to a song.

2.

"*Candelabrum,* Can-de-la-brum" comes
Like a chant to Maxine Schumate
Entranced by the assonance of the word.
Short *a*'s and short *e*'s become a dance
Of shadows in her mind. "C-A-N-D," she begins,
And her eyes comb the countenance
Of the announcer, search for mnemonic
Signals to keep her in the fold.
It isn't even a competition really; the more bodies
Left on stage, the less the spotlight blooms
Or glowers. In the audience, the clenched-
Hearted parents sit in the dark. Alone and black,
   How can I stand in so much light?
   How can I stand in all this darkness?

On Stage

The Akron Armory is filled to capacity with more than 2,000 peo-
ple; mostly parents, sitting with hats in laps, with fidgeting eyes,
with hands held, in a space seldom found gorged for circuses, box-
ing, or wrestling, but tonight people are here to see teenagers
spell. Tonight, tethered to the stage, the crowd listens as if a great
light commanded their attention, as if the stage were on fire, as if
the whole world, all at once, were trying to utter one word.

One word? Spelling is a war of letters, syllables, utterances, and
inflections. It would only take a second to end a year's worth of
work: maybe you didn't hear the announcer, maybe you conjured
a homophone of the word, maybe you felt underdressed for the
lights and applause, maybe a whippin' awaited you at home after
you tripped on a letter, maybe you just didn't give a damn, but
you were trapped there and so was the crowd; maybe you cared,
but you were tired and the crowd was hungry; maybe you knew
this would always be the crowning moment of your life, but you
couldn't sustain it. It's like that sometimes; sometimes the
weight is too heavy to lift one word, one letter, off the tongue.

But you start seeing yourself spelling before the crowd. You envi-
sion the competition as if it were a dream: the stage begins to
clear, the field is narrowing down, the competition is falling, and,
instead of gaining confidence you gain weight; you feel as if
you're being inflated on stage and the more space left on this
spotlit landscape, the more you fill it in with your flesh. The

crowd is moving back, the stage is shrinking beneath your toes, the ceiling is lifting; you see, for the first time, there is a sky above your sky; you raise an arm to reach it and the crowd gasps, you stretch and the crowd shrieks. You try to float to the sky in this inflated, brown body through the hole that used to be a ceiling by raising your arms, but then you hear the announcer, who is bigger than you, who is twice your size, to whose crotch you now stand, who starts spitting words at you; his tongue is forked like a cross-road; his head is red and shaped like a thimble—ostensibly, he has no neck; and he continues spitting words for you to spell as accurately as you can. But he doesn't want you to spell them, really; he's spitting words to find *the* word that will eliminate you; *the* word that you did not memorize among the 100,000 on the list; *the* word large enough, contorted enough to choke you. The announcer has a bulge under his jacket. You don't know what will happen if you make a mistake. You move from word to word.

But this is not the dream. You find that the crowd is actually supportive; they want to see you spell—not see you spell in a circus-act way, mind you, but in an adult-looking-at-a-child-in-wonderment way—and they will applaud when you open your mouth, when you say Yes sir, No sir; they will applaud when the announcer says, That's correct, and they will applaud when you think you can't go any further for the applause. And then you realize you're not alone; you hear John Huddleston, a tall, white teen from St. Vincent-St. Mary's, trumpet through *Sciatic*, but stumble on *Cocklebur*, but you don't do any better and then before Maxine Schumate tries to spell *Candelabra*, she asks the announcer to repeat it, *Candelabra,* as if it were the magic words to a potion. Maxine. Poor Maxine Schumate: she is now the victim of your dream. She transposes the *l* and the *e.* You see smoke coming from her mouth, you see flames where her eyes used to set and then you don't see her. Vanished. You're happy. She walks off the stage into the shadow of shaking heads and consolations. You're happy? And she now thinks that this wasn't worth it anyway. You're happy? And she will never compete again. You're happy? As the shadows and backstage curtains swallow her whole. You're happy? As her face is now upholstered with embarrassment. But, for now, you must keep your head up and rejoice because you're standing on stage in front of 4,000 blue eyes filled with awe, eyes that are now fixed on you. The crowd starts leaning in; the crowd is no longer an audience; the crowd is showing its teeth; the crowd is a proud parent, smiling; the crowd hears the words of the announcer as clearly as you do: *voluble, vol-u-ble,* he repeats. Can you spell it? A voice asks. *Can I spell it?* A voice whispers. Voluble, V-O-L-U- . . . The letters vaporize through the armory and between each one you think of everything you must think about to get through one word.

Say the letters clearly so they don't think all Negro girls have thick tongues; don't give them a reason to stop letting people like you compete, they already know you're not smart enough; don't confirm it by losing; don't look unkempt; I told you to soak in the tub before you go on stage; I told you don't stay in the sun too long the week before you go on stage; you don't want to look too black under those lights on stage; change your draws before you go on stage; polish your shoes with Kiwi black; brush your teeth with baking soda; moisten your skin with cocoa butter; I wish you would go on stage ashy; don't go on stage ashy; I wish you would go on stage crying; don't go on stage crying; keep your back erect even if you miss a word; keep your back erect, even if they call you a word you don't like; tell me you know what fork to use; tell me you wore a slip under that dress; tell me that's ribbon in your hair; tell me you washed your hair and used oil; tell me you know the winning word; you gotta listen when they say the word; you gotta repeat it so they know you know it; let me hear you spell it like there are no more words left to spell: voluble, V-O-L-U-B-L-E.

MacNolia Backstage with Fats Waller
And Bill Robinson at the RKO Palace Theater

Cleveland, 1936

1. *Fats*

Girl, if you don't know this dance, this beat
Under the soles of turned-over shoes,
How a spine stands like an exclamation point

Despite the hard times,
How kisses bloom on the back of your hand,
Your own swagger, your own sway,

Your own grammar, your own name,
How to dance the Eagle Rock, Lulu,
Jitterbug, Waltz with thorns in your feet,

Temptation when he tugs on your elbow,
Temptation when he lowers his eyes and walks away,
An audience jazzing your name

As you move from shadows to light—
If you don't know how your own innocence
Ain't engraved in stone—

I mean, you ought to know, experience wears
Down its hard edges, and neither will leave you alone—
Soon, you have to learn, they both live under your skin,

Young enough to lift their skirts
And dance like nobody's business.

2. *Bojangles*

tell me   you can't   hear
survival songs,   journeys traveled,

wars and   love won,
under the   soles of

these feet,   under the
beat of   these steel

heels. there's   a world
lying like   a body

at rest   waiting, like
opportunity   never will,

for a   girl like   you to
pop open   the top   and see

what's underneath   it all.
it's not   going to   come up

and tap   you on   those brown
shoulders and   ask to   dance,

it's   gonna run   away and hide
every chance   it gets,   but baby

you' just   gonna have   to put
on your   running shoes   and spread

those nostrils   like a   hellhound on
the heels   of a   man who

made   a deal   with the   devil,
you' gonna   have to   dance like

your life, your rent,   your breakfast
lunch and   dinner depended   on how

fast you   click your   heels; and   then,
once   you make   it—i mean   once you

really make   it happen   for you—
you had   better remember   where you

came from   'cause there   will be
days you   have to   find your   way back

and you   realize your   journey is
always shorter   when you'   headed home

'cause as   long as   you' headed out
for what   this world   has to

offer but   refuses to   unfold her
fist for   you to   take, you

realize you   gotta lift   your knees
and pump   your elbows,   baby,   'cause

no matter   how good   you be,
or even   how good   you get,

hellhounds is   always gonna   be after   you, too.

My Dream of Charon

Comes to me in a breath,
Faster than I bat my eyes at a boy,
And I wonder how does he
Know who will cross and who
Will wait a 100-year spell
When he moves more like light
Than the penumbra of what
Once was man. How could his silhouette
Shine through this fog?
How does he comb over our spirits
Without a second thought?
What does his marriage
To death tell him about my life?
Why are his eyes—blacker than the river Styx,
Hotter than gold coins—fixed on me
When I'm just trying to find
My way to school?

Details Torn from MacNolia's Diary

May 25, 1936

Morning: What's another word for *rage* if not *loss?*

Set out for boat ride on the Wilson Line

With other district champs, but not allowed above

The bottom of the boat. History in my nostrils, flared.

A pigeon asked me for a quarter

In the park. A beggar ate crumbs from my hand.

Lunch: White House. Washington Monument in background,

Mother and Ms. Norris in foreground. *Chiaroscuro*, a word

I must remember. Elizabeth Kenney is a Negro girl

From a southern district, somewhere in North Carolina.

She's wringing her hands. I must keep my head. Everything moves

Like it's from a different planet. Street vendors have more hands

Than Vishnu. No one is in love in DC. Where do the babies

Come from in this town? No, how do they survive? An old,
   Negro

Man is dancing in the middle of the street; he moves his gloved
   hand

East, and the cars move toward the sun, he moves his other hand

West, and they head toward the ocean. Someone loves him who
   walks

The dotted line. How else does he get his shoes off at night?

Night: my hand disappears inside President Roosevelt's as he

Congratulates me, just for showing up, before the competition.

Elizabeth Kenney misspells *Appellation* in round one.

Now, I'm alone and the dreams set in:

I see Ethel Waters pouring tea at a table in the audience.

Was Asa Philip Randolph really shining shoes in the lobby?

I ask again, where do the babies come from? And I'm snapped

Back to the spelling bee as the announcer repeats *Nemesis*

As two tongues dance like a poor child for change

Behind his teeth.

MacNolia

National Spelling Bee Championship Montage[1]

May 24–26, 1936

Train Station, Akron, Ohio

This, my first train ride—
Whether it takes me to love
Or just the unknown—
This an open gate to me
This an open gate to me. . . .

        How should I regard
        What I've prepared so long for?
        With questions? Guesses?
        No, I've done my job and well.
        Now, who dares to judge my fate?

There's a song that goes,
The gospel trains a comin',
I hear jus' at hand,
I hear the car wheels rumblin',
An' rollin' over the land.

---

1. MacNolia placed fifth in the nation and won a seventy-five-dollar prize.
Although it couldn't be proved, it was rumored that the judges "set out to knock
MacNolia from the bee" by choosing an unapproved word, "nemesis." Jean
Trowbridge won the bee on the word "interning." *Beacon Journal,* May 21, 2000.

Crossing Maryland State Line

What looks more lonely
Than a train depot after
A train pulls off?
Maybe it's me plucked from my
Seat, propped in a colored car.

When white men see kids
What, pray tell, do they see? Black
Threat of revenge lit
With my young darkness? My rage?
Rage? I have yet to learn it.

What words help define
The official tone this man
Uses against my
Mom and me? I wish she had
Stayed home and simply prayed.

Hamilton Hotel, Washington, DC

*District Spelling Champs
Enter Here*, read one banner
Over front entrance,
Hamilton Hotel; *Colored
Door in Back*, read the other.

How elitist! A
Door, stairwell, table and chair
All set up for me.
Did I deserve all this fuss?
All for one little, black girl.

Façade is façade:
Carpet, wallpaper, tables
And chairs, chandeliers . . .
All is veneer—all fears stem
From a smudge on the surface.

The Home of Dr. T. Edward Jones

Life blooms under his
Roof. *Sanctuary*, now I
Know the spelling and
The meaning of the word, here
Where we find definition.

He can name and spell
My body: every bone,
Muscle, organ, cell.
He can lay hands and heal sick
Women and babies and men.

Who would deny *him*
A seat at the front of the
Bus, or along the
Counter, or at the table
Where Jesus, himself, kept faith?

National Museum, Washington, DC, Championship Day

How can they ask my
Mother to climb these back stairs
With swollen ankles?
I wish I had left her home:
I never would have told her.

    Countenance tells more
    Than words, and these faces spell
    Hate. As if I'm here
    To steal something from them, like
    Praise and love were white only.

And what if I win?
Does it make them any less
Or me more? It's sad
To think a competition
Of words could sharpen one's teeth.

National Museum Auditorium,

I sit alone.
I am *Job*, a leper, skin
But not flesh, flesh but
Not soul, soul but not human,
Human but not equal being.

The whites misspell words
But they can find alternate
Spellings from Mr.
Webster, their friend, my friend who
Now seems a long-sleeved dealer.

Mr. Webster is
The devil. He never taught
Me how to spell
Ne-muh-sis but now I know
What she's all about.

Train Station, Washington, DC, Train Ride Home

The people will want
To know what happened: the word
Was not on the list,
But *Nemesis* is common
Usage—at least, in the South.

But is it really
Any better at home where
They smile as they pull
The blade out of your backside?
Where love can be deceptive?

Through the train window
Whole worlds pass by so quickly
I can only squint,
Only allow so much light—
To watch it all blurs the heart.

Train Station, Akron, Ohio, Arrival Back Home

In the crowd, tears fall
But are wiped with much applause.
I recognize pain,
But there is also joy
Blooming on a brown boy's face.

People waving flags,
People throwing confetti,
People who don't care,
People kissing in the rain,
Ignoring the grayest clouds.

N-e-m-e-s-i-s Blues

I'd rather have no name, no name for my man to call
Say, I'd rather lose my name, no name to call
Than to use my name to make a poor girl crawl

They gon' and used my name, cruel as they can be
They up and broke my good name, cruel as they can be
Done set fire to my name and blown the smoke back at me

Smells like turpentine is in the drinks tonight
Yeah, *put* some turpentine in the drinks tonight
Might as well get crazy cause we gonna have to fight

My name must taste like a misspelled word
Poor girl, my name must taste like a misspelled word
But when it's all over, I'll show 'em how trouble gets stirred

Than to use my name to make a poor girl crawl
Man, I'd rather have no name, no name for my man to call
Hell, I'd rather *lose* my name, have no name at all

In Allan Rohan Crite's
School's Out

Bodies of women cut off
At the edge of canvas.
The orange undertone and
Yellow dresses are summer.
Buildings stand through brick
And mortar; the girls skip
Through sinew and bone.
The streets teem with saddle shoes,
Ankle socks, ribbons, bows,
Doilies, and breath. It's not so
Odd, their being without men
And boys, but what of the four
White girls in the background;
And what of the oil-and-sand-
Faced women, the pride in their
Breasts, butts, and strides? And
What can be said of the one
Who stands in the absurd center
Of this scene, wondering where
To, now? Their faces have no smiles—
Like curtains ajar to dark windows—
But their eyes are wise, which is why
The girls who teeter at the edge
Of the canvas, running full stride,
Draw questions
To the world, and the possibilities,
They have yet to enter.

My One White Friend

Asks the question that stings
More than the truth of the situation:
You don't think they did that to you
Just because you're a Negro, do you?
And then she answers herself
Knowing my response simply would
Not do: *I don't think they would have*
Let you get that far just to set you up.
An electric breath fills my chest.
For the first time
I notice how blonde her hair flows,
How blue her eyes, how thin her lips,
Which have just separated us forever.

Mabel Norris, Reporter
for the Akron Beacon Journal[1]

Covering the Spelling Bee

Murder had not been committed—
I broke the last one wide open,
Even scooped the *Cleveland*
Plain Dealer—so the men thought,
Sure, let her cover the spelling bee.
And I thought, *Yeah, let me; I'll show them.*

But I didn't have to convince them
As much as myself; the bee
Had become big news, as I thought
It would once I realized even Cleveland
Hadn't had a Negro to win, which opened
The rabbit hole for anyone committed

To the truth. I felt relegated to this beat
Because I was a woman, but found,
From God, a higher purpose: I could use my voice
To speak up for another, one usually not heard.
MacNolia Cox, the girl who won,
Needed a supporter who could speak

---

1. Mabel Norris, a reporter for the Akron *Beacon Journal* in 1936, accompanied
MacNolia and her mother to the National Spelling Bee. Norris protested when
the Southern judges chose "nemesis" for MacNolia to spell, which was not on the
approved list of words.

In a room full of white men who would speak
Over her, or any other Negro, whether she won
Or lost; it didn't really matter. Being heard
Was not easy for any woman, but a white voice,
Even as a female, could, at least, be found
Among a roomful of brutes, alone, trying to beat

Their arguments to the ground. Love
Was not on the agenda, not for the national
Competition, at least. In Akron, I'm proud
To say, she did have a chance,
Which, when you think about it, should
Be plenty, but it's only enough

When having a fair deal is enough
To win. And, I'm telling you, she should
Have won it all, but a fair chance
Was far from her lips. Her mother was proud
To see her standing under those national
Flashbulbs and spotlights until the love

Of a mother was the only rope the poor girl
Had to hold onto, the only one
Not already knotted into a noose.
The white district champs would offer
Alternate spellings, contest pronunciations,
Be given chances. Not MacNolia. She had to spell

And make it as crisp as a virgin's bed. Spell
Like mankind depended on her voice to pronounce
Us all among the living, as if fallen angels offered
Hell or salvation, a woman's womb or a ready noose.
We knew the odds didn't promise much: one
Utterance trips off the tongue of a girl

Against a wind that started blowing
Centuries before she was even born,
But carrying her name, nonetheless, one letter
At a time. Even in the final round when they sat
Her down—when the announcer pulled *Nemesis*
From up his sleeve—if she didn't win that night . . .

My God, if she didn't win that night.

Fin

"This is just the beginning for her."
  Arlena Bauford, president
    Akron Chapter of the National Council of Negro Women

from "MacNolia Cox Wins," Akron *Beacon Journal*,
April 23, 1936

"MacNolia Cox, who got discouraged and dropped out of school not long after [The National Spelling Bee, 1936], is now Mrs. John Montiere, and lives on W. North St. in Akron. She works for a doctor and his family."

from "How Bad It Used to Be," *Daytona Beach News-Journal*, June 3, 1971, Mabel Norris Chesley, associate editor

MacNolia's Dream of Shirley Temple

INTERIOR—JEFFERSON THEATER—NIGHT—
VOICE-OVER.

Twentieth Century Fox presents

Shirley Temple in *Just Around the Corner,* with

Bill Robinson as Corporal Jones—

LONG SHOT—CORPORAL JONES, the dancing doorman—
VOICE-OVER.

Bill Robinson's silver-soled feet
Translate a Morse code on the floor.
A fist is caught in his smile—

No, it's a smile caught in his fist,
Through a mouthful
Of copasetic and a-okay.

LONG SHOT—SHIRLEY—VOICE-OVER.

A movie in which Shirley is loved only

By the unloved, and even they

Need to be convinced—

CLOSE-UP of SHIRLEY's mouth.

God pinches the flesh
Here to cover a smile,
Then rubs his fingers over her lips,

Sticks a lollipop salve under her tongue.
She gives a cherry giggle.
Do we even need to note

The barrettes, the curls?
The hair, the eyes, the lips, the voice—
All conspire against me.

VOICE-OVER continues.

Here is a movie in which her mama is dead, her daddy

Is unemployed, she gets into a fight, wears

A handkerchief on her head, sings

"This Is a Happy Little Ditty," blackens

A wealthy white boy's eye, and is not

Liked by his parents, who,

Of course, fall in love with her

By the end once they realize

How smart she is, which is why I think

We have something in common,

Which is exactly what I'm *supposed* to believe—

Like the wealthy would open their homes

To the less-fortunate-but-cute class—as

I wonder how grand it must feel

To dance with Shirley and Mr. Robinson,

As I wonder how long he can hold

His smile, as I notice none of the girls

On screen look like me, but I think they should,

As the thought of me with Shirley—the very picture

Of me on stage—as I plant myself deeper into my seat—

Keeps me half waiting—half trembling—

For my name to roll in these credits.

IRIS IN—IRIS OUT.

CLOSE-UP—SHIRLEY.

*We PAN DOWN from SHIRLEY's face to feet, dancing,
while VO continues.*

How difficult is it to pick
On the white girl in gold curls,
In pastel ribbons? Don't you see

The twinkle in her eye is really
A wince; the lollipop, just
Some thing to bite down on; her

Dance—her awkward little dance,
Her shuck and jive—
A marionette's lift of the leg

And cock of the head for
Her fans, her mama, the studio,
And, I admit, for me?

Now, with more of her past to comb,
What do you love,
When what you loved, really,

Had no future?

Acknowledgments

I'd like to thank the editors of the following publications, in which some of these poems first appeared. *Crab Orchard Review*: "MacNolia's Dream of Shirley Temple." *CUE: A Journal of Prose Poetry*: "On Stage," "to," and "John Montiere *answer to question three*." *The Georgia Review*: "from." *The Holland Sentinel*: "MacNolia Cox Meets John Montiere." *nocturnes*: "Dust," "Akron Spelling Bee." *Poetry Daily* (www.poems.com): "from." *Poetry 30: An Anthology of Thirty Poets in Their Thirties*: (reprint) "The Night Richard Pryor Met Mudbone." *Printed Matter* (Japan): "MacNolia Backstage with Fats Waller and Bill Robinson at the RKO Palace Theater." *Rivendell*: "The Night Richard Pryor Met Mudbone." *Seneca Review*: "Death Letter Blues Ghazal."

Appreciation is also given to Warren Wilson College and the MFA Program for Writers for the 2000–2001 Joan Beebe Graduate Teaching fellowship, during which many of these poems were completed, and to the 2002 Cave Canem Workshop.

Akron, Ohio, research: Annette Blakney; Georgia Gay, who is MacNolia's niece; Nate and Yvonne Oliver; Mark J. Price; Laura Walker; and my family. Also thanks to the late Dr. Shirla McClain for her dissertation *Contributions of Blacks in Akron*.

Appreciation is given for the suggestions, readings and support from the following: Elizabeth Alexander; Brian Bardwell; Laure-Anne Bosselaar; Tammy Brown; Chin Chong; Michael Collier;

Stuart Dischell; Toi Derricotte; Cornelius Eady; Nikki Finney; Reginald Gibbons; Jennifer Grotz; Terrance Hayes; Kristin Henderson; Bob Holman and The Bowery Poetry Club; Melissa Hotchkiss; Jesse Ingram; Sandra Jackson and The Studio Museum of Harlem; Honoree Jeffers; Meta Duewa Jones; Yusef Komunyakaa; Toni Asante Lightfoot; Carolyn Micklem; Sarah Micklem; E. Ethelbert Miller; David Mills; Reza Namdar; Marilyn Nelson; Lyn O'Hare; Patrick Phillips; Joel Dias Porter; Martha Rhodes; Yanick Rice-Lamb; Heather Sellers; Richard, Eula and Felicia Shaw; giovanni singleton and *nocturnes;* Chezia Thompson; and Al Young.

Thanks to Sebastian Matthews, Peter Turchi and Ellen Bryant Voigt for having faith.

Special thanks to Lucinda Bartley and Carol Houck Smith for making this book possible.